W9-CFB-080

Scott Foresman

# Decodable Practice Readers 16A - 30C

## Volume 2

Scott Foresman
is an imprint of

PEARSON

Glenview, Illinois • Boston, Massachusetts • Chandler, Arizona
• Upper Saddle River, New Jersey

**Copyright © by Pearson Education, Inc., or its affiliates.** All Rights Reserved. Printed in the United States of America. This publication is protected by copyright, and permission should be obtained from the publisher prior to any prohibited reproduction, storage in a retrieval system, or transmission in any form or by any means, electronic, mechanical, photocopying, recording, or likewise. For information regarding permissions, write to Pearson Curriculum Group Rights & Permissions, One Lake Street, Upper Saddle River, New Jersey 07458.

Pearson, Scott Foresman, and Pearson Scott Foresman are trademarks, in the U.S. and/or other countries, of Pearson Education, Inc., or its affiliates.

ISBN-13: 978-0-328-49218-3
ISBN-10: 0-328-49218-3

10 V011 14 13 12

CC1

## UNIT 4

Decodable Practice Reader 16A
**The Lunch Table** ..... 1

Decodable Passage 16B
**Anna's Fable** ..... 9

Decodable Practice Reader 16C
**The Maple Tree** ..... 11

Decodable Practice Reader 17A
**A Good Book** ..... 19

Decodable Passage 17B
**Cookbooks** ..... 27

Decodable Practice Reader 17C
**Kevin Hooks a Fish** ..... 29

Decodable Practice Reader 18A
**Joy's Flowers** ..... 37

Decodable Passage 18B
**Troy's Flowers** ..... 45

Decodable Practice Reader 18C
**Cowboy Roy** ..... 47

Decodable Practice Reader 19A
**Boyhood Dreams** ..... 55

Decodable Passage 19B
**Jack's Daydreams** ..... 63

Decodable Practice Reader 19C
**Joy's Raincoat** ..... 65

Decodable Practice Reader 20A
**Is It True?** ..... 73

Decodable Passage 20B
**Sally's New Puppy** ..... 81

Decodable Practice Reader 20C
**New Clues** ..... 83

## UNIT 5

Decodable Practice Reader 21A
**Restful Hobbies** ..... 91

Decodable Passage 21B
**Victor's Birthday** ..... 99

Decodable Practice Reader 21C
**The Helpful Gardener** ..... 101

Decodable Practice Reader 22A
**In the Woods** ..... 109

Decodable Passage 22B
**Betty's Medal** ..... 117

Decodable Practice Reader 22C
**An Unhappy Spaceman** ..... 119

Decodable Practice Reader 23A
**Writing Letters** ..... 127
Decodable Passage 23B
**Camp Gnome** ..... 135
Decodable Practice Reader 23C
**Meet Tom Lamb** ..... 137
Decodable Practice Reader 24A
**Phil's Zoo Fun** ..... 145
Decodable Passage 24B
**Gramps' Photos** ..... 153
Decodable Practice Reader 24C
**Photos from Ted** ..... 155
Decodable Practice Reader 25A
**Fun in August** ..... 163
Decodable Passage 25B
**Dawn's Daughter** ..... 171
Decodable Practice Reader 25C
**A Job for Paul** ..... 173

## UNIT 6

Decodable Practice Reader 26A
**The Nicest Surprise** ..... 181

Decodable Passage 26B
**Zoo Fun** ..... 189

Decodable Practice Reader 26C
**The Happiest King** ..... 191

Decodable Practice Reader 27A
**Mrs. Jenkins** ..... 199

Decodable Passage 27B
**Titles** ..... 207

Decodable Practice Reader 27C
**North Hall Street** ..... 209

Decodable Practice Reader 28A
**My Future** ..... 217

Decodable Passage 28B
**Future Profession** ..... 225

Decodable Practice Reader 28C
**Action at the Game** ..... 227

Decodable Practice Reader 29A
**Helpless Randy** ..... 235

Decodable Passage 29B
**An Incredible Visit** ..... 243

Decodable Practice Reader 29C
**In the Darkness** ..... 245

Decodable Practice Reader 30A
**Hiking the Hard Way** ..... 253

Decodable Passage 30B
**Wrong!** ..... 261

Decodable Practice Reader 30C
**The Midtown Market Sale** ..... 263

# The Lunch Table

Written by Laura Susin

Decodable Practice Reader 16A

**Final Syllable *-le***

| | | | |
|---|---|---|---|
| simple | table | able | purple |
| sparkle | handle | puddle | bundle |
| tickle | candle | giggle | |

**High-Frequency Words**

| | | |
|---|---|---|
| set | table | today |
| able | water | |

It's time to eat.
It is simple to set this table.
Pam is able to do it
by herself.

First, Pam sets purple dishes
on her table.
Pam likes purple.
Today is a nice day for purple.

Pam sets glasses on the table.
They sparkle in the sunlight.
Pam gets napkins too.
Her napkins match the purple plates.
It is fun setting the table!

Pam holds the jug of
water by the handle.
She will not spill.
There will be no puddle!

This table needs
a bundle of roses.
Won't this table smell nice?
Roses tickle Pam's nose!

Last, this table needs a candle on it.
Mom will light that candle.
After that, Mom can finish
making lunch.
Pam can't wait to eat!

The table is set.
Mom sets lunch on the table.
Pam and Mom fixed lunch as a team!
It makes Pam giggle to think
of how she was able to help.

# Anna's Fable

Decodable Practice Passage 16B

**Final Syllable *-le***

| | | | |
|---|---|---|---|
| Tuttle | Fables | simple | riddles |
| puzzles | settled | table | little |
| turtle | fiddle | maple | juggle |
| pebbles | single | nibble | bubble |
| trickle | able | struggle | |

**High-Frequency Words**

| | | | |
|---|---|---|---|
| table | today | turn | want |
| tree | find | water | able |
| show | | | |

Mister Tuttle is teaching fables in class. A fable is a tale that teaches a lesson. Some lessons might be simple. Some lessons may be more like riddles or puzzles. Last night, Anna settled in at her kitchen table.

Her homework was to make up a fable.

Today in class, it was Anna's turn to tell her fable. In her fable, a little turtle plays his fiddle rather than tackling winter chores. Turtle didn't want to work, just play that fiddle under his maple tree. Sometimes Turtle stopped fiddling just to juggle little pebbles. But when winter came, Turtle did not find a single thing to nibble, nor a bubble or trickle of water to drink.

In her fable, Anna is able to show that it is better to work hard in summer, than struggle in winter.

# The Maple Tree

Written by Kara Linden

Decodable Practice Reader 16C

**Final Syllable *-le***

| | | |
|---|---|---|
| maple | simple | stumble |
| table | bottle | bubbles |
| able | puddle | giggle |

**High-Frequency Words**

| | | |
|---|---|---|
| seen | tree | find |
| show | turn | want |

Have you seen that old maple tree?
It's simple to find the maple tree.
Stan can show the way!
He can run fast.
Can you?

Run by this big rock.
Do not stumble!
Turn right when you
pass this rock.

Kids are playing hopscotch.
It's not a hard game to play.
Run by that game.
Sit at that table.

It's time to rest!
We'll find the maple tree,
but first we'll drink the water
in this bottle.

Kids are blowing bubbles!
We will blow bubbles too.
Stan is able to blow big bubbles.

Off we go!
Jump over that big puddle
but don't step in.
Keep running.
The hardest part is over.

This is it!
This is the big maple tree for you to see.
We can sit under this tree.
We can giggle under this tree.
Why did you want to find this tree?

# A Good Book

Written by Quinn Hart

Decodable Practice Reader 17A

**Vowel Patterns *oo, u***

| | | | |
|---|---|---|---|
| book(s) | look | good | looking |
| stood | looked | cook | cookbook |
| took | put | full | |

**High-Frequency Words**

| | | | |
|---|---|---|---|
| get | book | for | these |
| ask | maybe | down | seat |

Mike has a card
that he uses to get books.
What kind of book
will he look for?

Mike runs up these steps.
He sees books, books,
and more books!
Can Mike find a good book?

Mike will ask the man at this desk.
"I'm looking for a book," Mike said.
"A book? We have lots of books!
What kind do you want?" he asked.

"I am looking for a good book,"
Mike said as he stood
and looked at books.
"Maybe I'll read this book.
It will teach me how to cook!"

Mike will check out this cookbook!
The man took Mike's card
and he took Mike's book.
Then he gave the book and card
back to Mike.

Mike put his bag down
and took a seat.
The book was full of good
things to eat.

Mike will take his book home.
He will cook with his mom!
Mike is on his way
to being a good cook!

# Cookbooks

Decodable Practice Passage 17B

**Vowel Patterns *oo, u***

| | | |
|---|---|---|
| butcher | Bush | cook |
| pushed | books | cooking |
| cookbooks | look | pudding |
| footlong | wood | pulled |
| took | put | nook |
| rookie | fulfilled | |

**High-Frequency Words**

| | | | |
|---|---|---|---|
| asked | for | maybe | book |
| box | down | these | lake |
| fish | get | seat | |

Sam the butcher finished his day's work at Mister Bush's store. Sam liked his job, but he asked Mister Bush for a job as a cook.

"Maybe," said Mister Bush. He pushed Sam to read books on

cooking. Sam took home a box of cookbooks.

On his way home that night, Sam sat down in his bus and looked at his books. These books told about cooking things from pudding to footlong hot dogs. His last book told him how to cook fresh lake fish on a wood fire.

The bus pulled into Sam's stop. He had to get up from his seat. Sam took his books home. He put them in his kitchen nook, but took one to read each day. In just weeks, Mister Bush gave Sam a job as a rookie cook!

Sam fulfilled his wish!

# Kevin Hooks a Fish

Decodable Practice Reader 17C

Written by Natalie Lohrman

**Vowel Patterns *oo, u***

| | | | |
|---|---|---|---|
| brook | full | shook | stood |
| look | hooks | put | hook |
| pulled | hooked | | |

**High-Frequency Words**

| | | |
|---|---|---|
| fish | let's | full |
| lake | box | |

Max and Kevin felt bored.
"Let's fish at the brook," said Kevin.
"No, let's fish at the lake,"
said Max.
"It is full of fish."

"Are the fishing poles
in this box?" asked Max.
Kevin shook the big box.
His poles fell out.
"Let's go," he said.

"Look!" yelled Kevin.
"The lake is close!
Let's race to that tree."
Kevin and Max ran to the tree
that stood by the lake.

Kevin and Max checked
their fishing hooks.
"Let's put our lines in," said Max.
They dropped the fishing lines in.

Kevin and Max stood for
a long time waiting for fish.
"When will those fish bite?"
asked Max.

Then there was a splash and a tug.
"I have a fish on my hook!"
yelled Kevin.
Kevin pulled hard on his line.

Kevin hooked a big lake fish!
When will Max hook a big
lake fish?

# Joy's Flowers

Written by Donyette Sanchez

Decodable Practice Reader 18A

**Diphthongs *ou, ow, oi, oy***

| | | |
|---|---|---|
| Joy | found | flower(s) |
| frown | soil | brown |
| now | how | pound |
| down | moist | shower |
| sprout | without | noise |
| out | ground | proud |

**High-Frequency Words**

| | | |
|---|---|---|
| seeds | soil | plant |
| land | brown | |

Joy found a bag of flower seeds.
What can she do with them?
Joy had a frown on her face.
Then she smiled.
She will make a garden in the soil!

What will she do first?
Joy will plant her seeds.
A good spot of land
is what Joy needs.

This soil is nice and brown.
Joy digs tiny holes
for the seeds.
She will dig holes
for every single one of them!

Now the seeds can be planted.
One seed in each hole
is how it's done.
Put soil on top,
but do not pound it down!

It's time to make the soil moist.
It is a shower for the flowers!
It will help them sprout.
Now they just need sunlight.

When will the flowers sprout?
Without a noise,
the flowers will poke out
of the ground and go up to the sky.

Joy is so proud!
Her flowers did get big.
She will pick one flower
and take it home.

# Troy's Flowers

Decodable Practice Passage 18B

**Diphthongs *ou, ow, oi, oy***

| | | | |
|---|---|---|---|
| Troy | boy | house | amount |
| brown | ground | pointed | found |
| counted | out | loud | choice |
| soil | outside | flowers | downtown |
| plowed | showered | moist | toil |
| sprout | proud | enjoy | |

**High-Frequency Words**

| | | |
|---|---|---|
| land | brown | wild |
| seeds | plant | soil |
| grow | | |

Troy was an older boy. Behind his house there was a large amount of land. It was good brown dirt filled with wild weeds. Troy pulled weeds out of that ground. He used a pointed weed puller he found.

Troy counted out loud as he pulled weeds.

Troy had a plan. A garden would be a good choice for the brown soil outside his house. Now that the weeds had been pulled out, flowers would be perfect!

Troy rode his bike downtown. He got seeds to plant in his brown soil. When he got back, he plowed the dirt a bit. Then Troy planted seeds. He showered his garden with water. Moist ground helped seeds grow.

Troy's toil paid off. Flowers began to sprout! Troy was proud! He would enjoy his flowers.

# Cowboy Roy

Written by Julia Parrish

Decodable Practice Reader 18C

**Diphthongs *ou, ow, oi, oy***

| | | |
|---|---|---|
| Roy | choice | cowboy(s) |
| around | ground | foil |
| cows | town | toys |
| spoiled | boy | joy |
| voice | join | noise |

**High-Frequency Words**

| | | |
|---|---|---|
| grow | speak | ride |
| rope | wild | |

"This is the day to tell
what you want to be
when you grow up!
Roy, will you speak first?"
the teacher asked.

What will Roy be?
Roy will tell the class his choice.
He will be a cowboy!

Roy will ride his horse around.
He will twirl his rope over
the ground.
He will herd those cows
and keep an eye on them.

Roy will protect the cows
from wild animals.
Maybe Roy will foil a plot
if some cows leave town.
He can save the herd!

Roy will give up his toys
to look after cows!
Roy is not a spoiled boy.
He thinks that being a cowboy
will bring him joy.

In his camp at night,
Roy will use his fine voice
to sing cowboy tunes
under the bright stars.

Yes! He will tell the class
how he will join other cowboys!
But Roy does not make a noise.
Roy is a very shy cowboy.

# Boyhood Dreams

Janis Jay

Decodable Practice Reader 19A

**Syllable Patterns**

| | | |
|---|---|---|
| boyhood | cowboy | Seaweed |
| daydreams | oatmeal | roundups |
| cookouts | Loudmouth | southeast |

**High-Frequency Words**

young
travel
direction
clear

Gramps told Gina about his boyhood dreams.
"When I was young, I dreamt about being a cowboy," he told her.

"I always saw myself riding an old horse named Seaweed," Gramps explained.
"Seaweed?" asked Gina.
"Yep," replied Gramps smiling.

"In my daydreams, I fed Seaweed oats.
I ate oatmeal.
Then we rode out on cattle roundups," added Gramps.

"We rode hard in daytime.
At night, we would enjoy cowboy cookouts," said Gramps.

"Did you ever try to be a real cowboy?" Gina asked.
"No, but once I rode an old horse," said Gramps with a bigger smile.

"This horse was named Loudmouth. I tried to travel in a southeast direction, but he didn't agree. So we rode northwest," said Gramps. Both he and Gina laughed.

"It was clear I would not be a good cowboy!" Gramps said to Gina
Gina hugged Gramps.
"But you are a great granddad," she said.

# Jack's Daydreams

Decodable Practice Passage 19B

**Syllable Patterns**

| | |
|---|---|
| railroads | daydream |
| cowboy | football |
| bookkeeper | railway |
| steamboat | sailboat |

**High-Frequency Words**

travel wide

At night, Mom and Jack planned to watch an old show about railroads. But as the show started, power in the house and on the whole block went out. It was a blackout!

Mom grabbed her flashlight. Jack sat outside on his porch. In the dark, Jack started to daydream about growing up. At first, he saw himself as a cowboy or a football player. He might make a good bookkeeper like his dad.

Jack remembered the show about railroads. He might work for a railway. Then he asked himself if there were still steamboats. He would like to travel by steamboat in a wide river. Or he might travel on a sailboat.

Jack's mind ran from idea to idea. That was the fun of daydreaming!

When that blackout ended, Jack stayed on the porch. Daydreaming was more fun than TV!

# Joy's Raincoat

Daniel Suh

Decodable Practice Reader 19C

**Syllable Patterns**

oatmeal raincoat
townhouse downtown
soybeans seaweed
rainbows

**High-Frequency Words**

clear several wide
street music

Mom packed Joy's lunch bag.
It had a sandwich, apple and
oatmeal bar.
"Thanks, Mom," yelled Joy as she ran
out to the school bus.

As Joy ran, Mom saw that Joy had a raincoat on her arm.
Mom looked out the townhouse window.
The day was sunny and clear!

When Joy stepped on the bus, kids saw that she held a raincoat. Several kids were afraid that might mean bad weather later.

The bus rode through wide downtown streets to Joy's school.
In class, Joy took her raincoat to her desk.
Miss Best spotted it and smiled.

Joy's class read about farms and soybeans.
It saw a DVD about seaweed.
Then Miss Best played music and kids painted rainbows.

At recess, kids waited in line to get a drink.
When kids hit the button, water sprayed them.
"They still didn't fix that!" said Miss Best.

That's when Joy put on her raincoat.
"I'm ready for a drink today," she said.
After her drink, Joy lent her raincoat to her classmates.

# Is It True?

Written by Meera Laurent

Decodable Practice Reader 20A

**Vowel Digraphs *oo, ue, ew, ui***

| | | | |
|---|---|---|---|
| Sue | true | moo | flew |
| moon | clue | too | |
| proof | drew | suit | |
| grew | soon | zoomed | |

**High-Frequency Words**

| | | |
|---|---|---|
| eyes | moon | another |
| picture | single | |
| only | thought | |

Sue needed to see
if it is true that a
cow that went "moo"
flew over the moon.

Sue will read to find a clue.
This book is full of cow facts.
But not a single cow flew!

Sue read about moon facts too.
It did not give proof that cows
ever came near the moon!

Sue had another clue
about what to do.
She asked an old cow
if she had ever flown over the moon.
That cow only said, "Moo."

Sue drew a picture of this cow.
She thought that wings
would suit the cow she drew.
Her hope grew that
she might soon learn if cows flew.

Sue waited and waited for
this cow to fly by.
But she soon grew tired
and her eyes closed tight.

Just as Sue started sleeping,
what do you think went by,
flying and leaping?
That cow zoomed
right over the moon!

# Sally's New Puppy

Decodable Practice Passage 20B

**Vowel Digraphs *oo, ue, ew, ui***

| | | | | |
|---|---|---|---|---|
| New | cool | Scoots | noon | moon |
| too | soon | chewing | blue | boot |
| shooed | juice | fruit | school | Woo |
| choose | drew | droopy | smooth | grooming |
| true | stoop | scoops | food | mood |

**High-Frequency Words**

| | | |
|---|---|---|
| new | moon | blue |
| thought | single | eyes |
| picture | gave | |

On Sunday, Sally got a new puppy. Cool! Sally named her puppy Scoots. Sally played with Scoots from noon until the moon shone in the sky. Bedtime came too soon!

When Sally woke the next day, Scoots was chewing her blue boot. "No Scoots!" Sally yelled as she shooed him away.

Sally had juice and fruit. In class, Miss Woo asked kids to draw. Sally thought for a single instant. That's all the time she needed to choose what to draw. Scoots!

Sally drew droopy eyes and a smooth nose. She drew fur that needed grooming. Her picture was true to life, too!

After school, Sally ran home. On her stoop, she heard Scoots barking in the house. Was he waiting for her?

Inside, Sally gave Scoots hugs and three scoops of food. Thanks to Scoots, Sally was in the best mood!

# New Clues

Written by Laura Nguyen

Decodable Practice Reader 20C

**Vowel Digraphs *oo, ue, ew, ui***

| | | | |
|---|---|---|---|
| clue | blue | room | broom |
| new | noon | food | cool |
| juice | tooth | bathroom | clues |

**High-Frequency Words**

| | | |
|---|---|---|
| hear | gave | blue |
| new | goes | |

I hear it go tick. I hear it go tock.
Mom gave me a clue
to find her blue timer.
It said, "Go to the room
with the big broom."

The room with the broom
had this new clue in place.
It said, "Go to the room
where you sit at noon."

At the table, this new clue waited.
"Find that place
that keeps food cool."

That freezer is cold!
That food and juice are frozen.
I took that clue out!
It told me to find that place
where each tooth is brushed!

That clue in the bathroom
asked me to find
the room with blue rugs.
Which room has blue rugs?

That's my room!
The timer goes
"tick, tock."
But I can't find it!

The timer went "ding!"
No new clues can be found.
Mom, show me where
the timer is now!

# Restful Hobbies

Written by Dennis Michaels

Decodable Practice Reader 21A

**Suffixes *-ly, -ful, -er, -or, -ish***

| | | | |
|---|---|---|---|
| gardener | gladly | peaceful | restful |
| painter | boldly | reddish | boastful |
| actor | gladly | stylish | storyteller |
| weekly | playful | hiker(s) | bravely |
| teacher | | | |

**High-Frequency Words**

| | | |
|---|---|---|
| free | enjoy | garden |
| anything | place | |

Most people have a hobby.
A hobby is something people do
in their free time to have fun.
What hobbies can you enjoy?

Janet is a gardener.
She tends her plants gladly.
She thinks her garden is a
peaceful place.
Making plants grow is restful
for Janet.

Kelvin is a painter.
He boldly uses bright colors.
His paintings are reddish in color.
His paintings are very good,
but Kelvin is not boastful
about his skills.

Cathy is an actor.
She acts in plays.
Cathy gladly tells stories on stage
through her fine acting.
She likes wearing stylish costumes.

Ben is a storyteller too,
but he does not act on stage.
He leads a weekly story time
at a little book store.
Kids like his playful readings.

Tess is a hiker.
She has finished long trails.
She has bravely hiked up peaks.
Tess is a good teacher for
new hikers.

Anything can be a hobby.
It can be dance, reading,
arts and crafts, or sports.
Just find something that makes
you happy and have fun!

# Victor's Birthday

Decodable Practice Passage 21B

**Suffixes *-ly, -ful, -er, -or, -ish***

| | | |
|---|---|---|
| older | joyful | happily |
| quietly | visitor | harmful |
| slowly | greenish | yellowish |
| closer | playful | quickly |

**High-Frequency Words**

| | | |
|---|---|---|
| told | teacher | you're |
| garden | anything | little |
| quickly | | |

It was Victor's birthday! In class, Victor told his teacher. She shook his hand. "You're getting older! Have a joyful day," she said happily.

Back home, Victor saw Mom chatting quietly with a visitor in the garden. When Mom spotted Victor, she pointed at a flower. "A harmful bug is on that flower," she said slowly. "It's greenish with yellowish wings."

Victor looked closer. He didn't see anything. And he didn't see Mom give the visitor a playful wink.

"Whoops, Victor! That little bug flew into the backyard," Mom said excitedly. "Go look quickly!"

Victor ran to the back. He found Dad standing next a greenish bike. It had yellowish wings painted on it!

Suddenly, Victor guessed that the visitor was a delivery person. The greenish and yellowish thing was really a bike. It was Victor's birthday gift!

# The Helpful Gardener

Written by Jan Stroud

Decodable Practice Reader 21C

**Suffixes *-ly, -ful, -er, -or, -ish***

| | | | |
|---|---|---|---|
| brightly | skillful | gardener | peaceful |
| helpful | hardly | quickly | helper |
| weekly | teacher | gently | hopeful |
| fondly | tightly | closely | selfish |
| sweetly | thankful | visitor | |

**High-Frequency Words**

| | | |
|---|---|---|
| quickly | teacher | told |
| learns | you're | little |

"The sun shines brightly,"
Kim said to herself.
Kim's mom is a skillful gardener.
Sunny days are spent helping
Mom in her peaceful garden.

Kim is helpful.
She can hardly wait.
She quickly runs
to Mom's garden.
Kim is a good helper.

Kim and her mom work
in the garden weekly.
Kim learns from her mom.
"You're a good teacher,"
Kim told her mom.

Mom tends big plants.
Kim tends little plants.
When plants look weak,
Kim gently nurses each plant.

Mom and Kim are hopeful.
This garden is growing well.
"This may be the best garden
we have grown," Mom said,
fondly patting Kim's cheek.

Kim hugs her mom tightly.
Then she gets back to her work.
"To be a good gardener like Mom,
I will watch closely and work hard,"
Kim said. "I can't be selfish."

Kim smiles sweetly.
She is thankful for this garden.
"Every visitor will like this garden,"
she thought.

# In the Woods

Written by Paula Bilika

Decodable Practice Reader 22A

**Prefixes *un-, re-, pre-, dis-***

| | | | |
|---|---|---|---|
| unlocks | unload | precooked | unties |
| unpacks | unhooks | unsafe | relight |
| unrolls | repack | dislikes | |

**High-Frequency Words**

| | | |
|---|---|---|
| family | swim | hills |
| them | night | soft |

Kenny and his family
like to go to the woods.
They camp in tents.
They swim in the lake
and hike in the hills.

Kenny unlocks the car.
He helps his mom pack.
Dad drives them to a good spot.
Then they unload tents,
full backpacks, and precooked food.

Kenny unties the ropes on the tent.
He helps his mom and dad
set up the tents.
Then Dad unpacks the food
and sets out a yummy dinner.

Kenny likes fishing at the lake.
If Dad gets a tiny fish, he unhooks
it and puts it back in the lake.
Those fish are too little to keep.

Mom puts water on the campfire
when they go hiking.
"It is unsafe to let it burn,"
Mom tells Kenny.
"We can relight it later."

At night, Kenny unrolls
his soft sleeping bag and slips in.
Sleep will feel good
after his full day
of hiking, fishing, and swimming.

It's time to repack the car.
Kenny dislikes litter,
so he cleans up the campsite.
He doesn't overlook anything.
Kenny can't wait to come back!

# Betty's Medal

Decodable Practice Passage 22B

**Prefixes *un-, re-, pre-, dis-***

| | | |
|---|---|---|
| unpacked | unable | unlike |
| rethought | unhappy | disliked |
| preteen | retrace | unfolded |
| rewrapped | unwrap | |

**High-Frequency Words**

| | |
|---|---|
| so | family |
| swim | soft |

When Betty unpacked, she was unable to find her medal. This was so unlike her. Betty rethought her steps. That didn't help. Unhappy Betty disliked asking her family for help, but she did!

"I'll find it," said Sally. "I saw a show about preteen kids that find things. I'm a preteen."

"Yes," said Betty.

"Let's retrace events since you won that medal at the swim meet," said Sally.

"I just did that!" said Betty.

Then Trish spoke up. She was three. "Betty, you looked happy when they gave you that medal."

"Yes," sighed Betty.

Trish gave Betty a soft, folded napkin. Betty unfolded it and found her medal!

"At home, I found that medal and rewrapped it," explained Trish. "I wanted you to unwrap it and be happy again!"

Betty hugged Trish, "I am happy!" she said.

# An Unhappy Spaceman

Written by Santi James

Decodable Practice Reader 22C

**Prefixes *un-, re-, pre-, dis-***

| | | | |
|---|---|---|---|
| preflight | dislikes | unlocks | reacts |
| unable | reclose | unmasks | unhappy |
| rewind | replay | reuse | |

**High-Frequency Words**

| | | |
|---|---|---|
| games | those | boys |
| space | so | come |

Jon and Jack like to
think up games.
Then they play them.
Most of the time those
boys are very silly.

Jon is playing a spaceman.
Jack will fly the space shuttle.
Their bedroom is a spaceship.
Jack does a preflight check
of the ship.

Jon pounds on the bedroom door.
Jack dislikes that noise.
Jack unlocks the door.
He reacts by jumping back
when he sees the spaceman.

Jack is unable to reclose his door.
What can he do so
that spaceman can't get him?
He hides behind his bed.

Then Jack acts brave.
He unmasks that unhappy spaceman.
Jack tells that spaceman to never
come back.
Jack has saved the day!

Mom and Dad got everything on film!
They rewind the film
and replay it so that
Jon and Jack can see.
Everyone laughs.

Next time Jon and Jack play,
Mom and Dad will reuse the tape
to make a funny new film.
Jon and Jack will be stars!

# Writing Letters

Written by Jamie Bernsen

Decodable Practice Reader 23A

**Consonant patterns *kn, wr, gn, mb***

| | | | |
|---|---|---|---|
| write | wrote | climbed | limb |
| knee | wrapped | numb | knights |
| knots | knit | writing | thumb |
| signed | | | |

**High-Frequency Words**

| | | |
|---|---|---|
| away | write | each |
| other | two | |

Fred has a friend named Dan.
Dan lives far away.
Fred and Dan write letters
and tell each other a lot.

Dan wrote a letter to Fred.
So Fred took out paper
and wrote a letter back to Dan.
He had a lot to tell him.

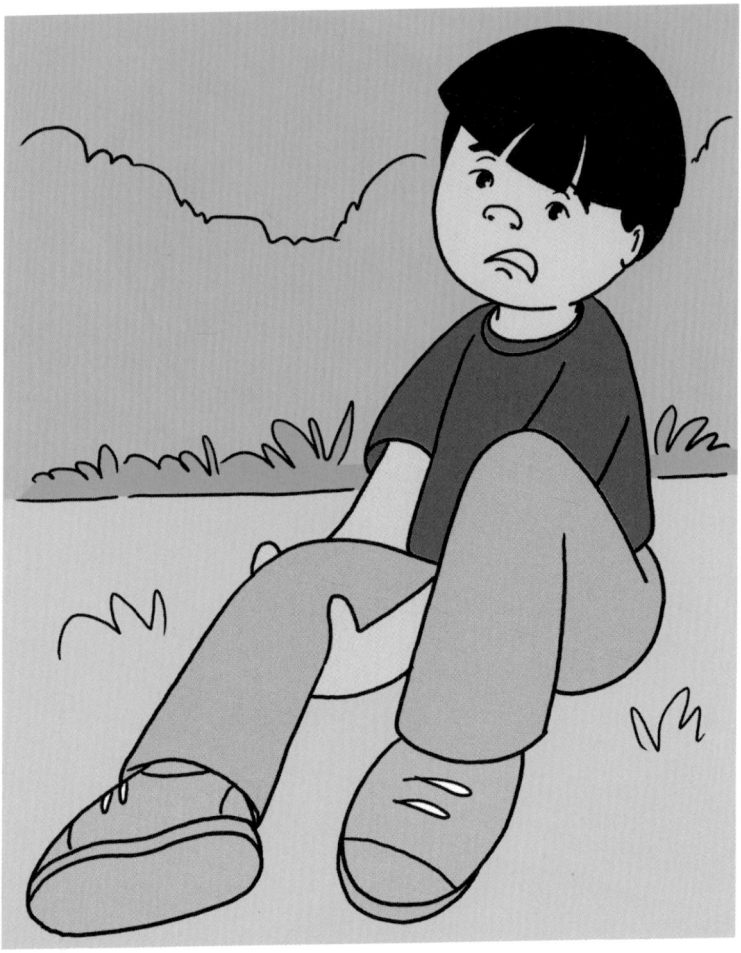

"I climbed a tree and
went out on a limb.
I fell and hurt my knee.
Mom wrapped it and put
ice packs on it to make it numb."

"After that, Mom got me
a new game with knights,
kings, and queens," Fred wrote.
"The knights ride horses."

Fred told Dan about his camping trip.
He told about the two cats
that Mom brought home.
"I like to watch them play
on the rug," Fred wrote.

Fred told Dan that he
is learning to tie knots.
His grandmother wants
to show him how to knit too.
"It looks like a fun hobby," Fred wrote.

Fred told Dan that he had
to stop writing.
"My thumb is hurting," he wrote.
He signed his letter
and added a note: "Write soon!"

# Camp Gnome

Decodable Practice Passage 23B

**Consonant Patterns *kn, wr, gn, mb***

| | | | |
|---|---|---|---|
| gnome | know | sign | designs |
| knew | write | climbed | knit |
| knee | wrap | wrong | Gnat |
| thumb | numb | | |

**High-Frequency Words**

| | | |
|---|---|---|
| know | other | write |
| man | who | |

Bruce spent a week at Camp Gnome. At first, he didn't know what a gnome was. But the camp sign showed an elf. A gnome was an elf! The camp had lots of other gnome stuff. It had gnome pictures, designs, and little stone gnomes.

Now Bruce really knew what a gnome was!

On his third night at camp, Bruce had to write home. He told Mom that he climbed a rope. He learned how to knit a gnome scarf, too! He told that he skinned his knee. The man who was in charge of camp helped wrap it.

As he wrote, bugs flew by his head. Bruce told Mom this place had the wrong name. It should be called Camp Gnat.

After writing a bit, Bruce's thumb went numb. He signed the letter and dropped in the gnome mailbox.

# Meet Tom Lamb

Written by Karen Vincent

Decodable Practice Reader 23C

**Consonant Pattern; *kn, wr, gn, mb***

| | | | |
|---|---|---|---|
| knocked | know | Lamb | wreath |
| sign | wrapped | wrench(es) | wrist |
| kneeled | knee | knob | wrong |
| knocking | | | |

**High-Frequency Words**

| | |
|---|---|
| truck | who |
| man | know |

An old, white truck
pulled into our driveway.
A man knocked
on our door.

"I know who that is," Dad said.
"It is Tom Lamb.
He has come to fix our pipes."
Dad let the man in.

"What are you making?" Tom asked as he pulled out his tools.
"It's a flower wreath," I said proudly. "I made a sign that has my name too."

Tom had his arm wrapped.
My dad asked if he had hurt it.
Tom said that he had hit it
with a wrench.
His wrist was still sore.

Tom had many wrenches.
He kneeled down,
put his knee on the ground,
then lay under the sink.
Tom turned a knob.

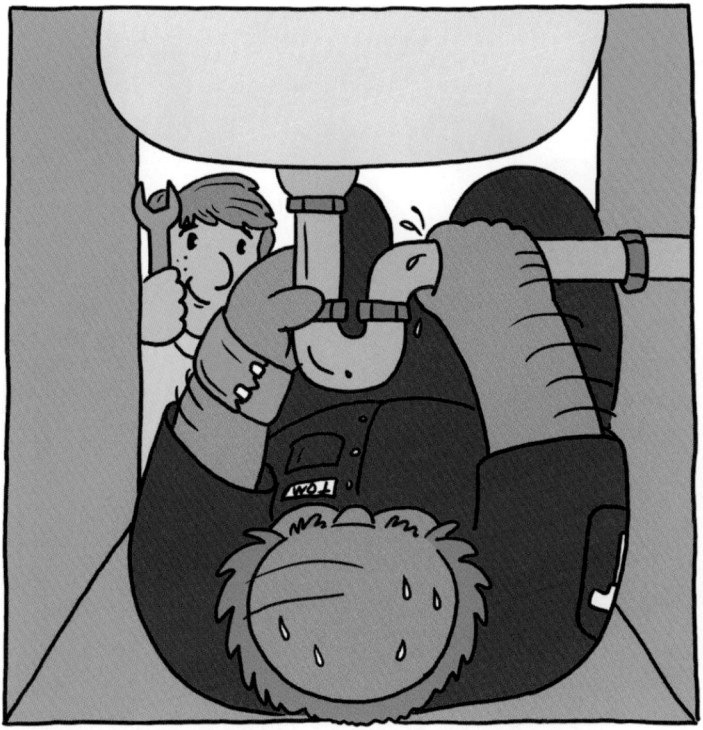

Clink! Clank!
"Oops!" Tom said. "Wrong pipe!"
I held a wrench for Tom
while he looked closer.

When my wreath was done,
I showed Dad and Tom Lamb.
Tom was finished too.
There was no more knocking
in the water pipes.

# Phil's Zoo Fun

Written by Alex Gardner

Decodable Practice Reader 24A

**Consonant Patterns; ph, gh, ck, ng**

| | | | |
|---|---|---|---|
| Phil | back | wrong | graph |
| sack | Phil's | photos | phrase |
| pick | singing | dolphin(s) | laughs |

**High-Frequency Words**

| | |
|---|---|
| animals | signs |
| happy | cool |

Phil likes animals.
Every summer, his mom and dad
take him back to the city zoo.
Phil can never go wrong
visiting that zoo.

First, they go in the petting zoo.
Phil likes petting the horses.
He feeds them hay.
A graph posted on the gate
shows how fast horses grow.

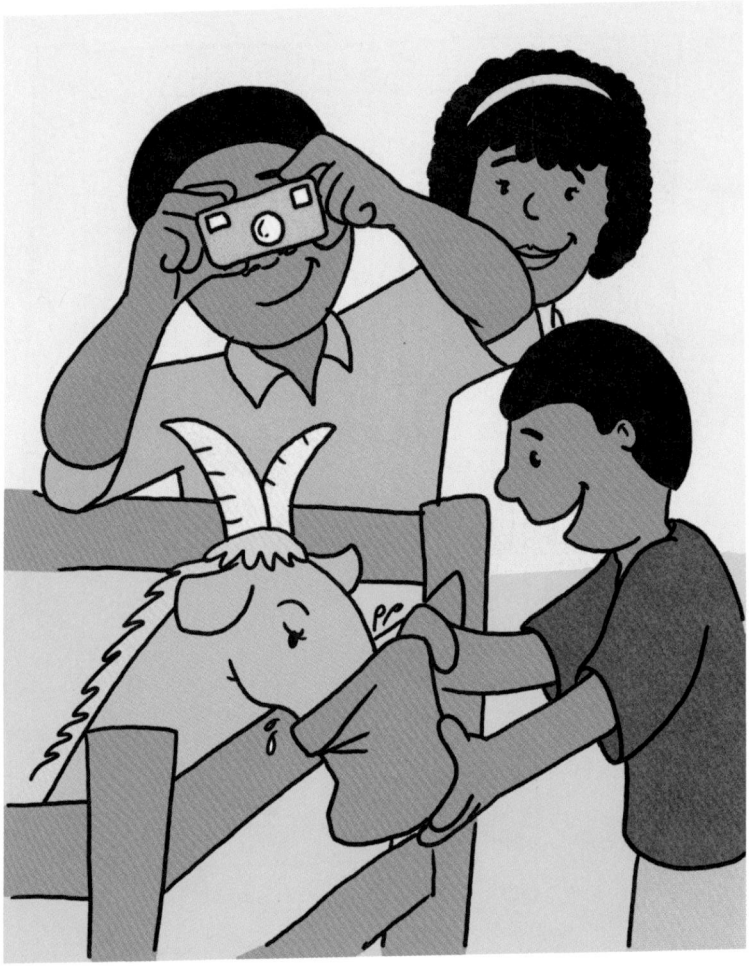

His mom gives him a sack.
It is stuffed with food
to feed the eager goats.
Those goats eat from Phil's sack.
His dad takes photos.

Phil pets a white
rabbit on the way out.
Next Phil visits wild animals.
He sees signs with the phrase
"Pick up litter!"

Hippos play in mud.
They look happy
by that cool stream.
Three foxes dart under bushes.
They are singing.

In the fish house,
Phil sees seastars, puffer fish,
sea horses, and sharks.
Phil likes to see
the sharks getting fed.

Before the zoo closes, Phil and his
mom and dad see a dolphin show.
The dolphins know how
to do fun tricks.
Splash! Everybody laughs.

# Gramps' Photos

Decodable Practice Passage 24B

**Consonant Patterns *ph, gh, ck, ng***

| | | | |
|---|---|---|---|
| Stephen | Phil | helping | photographs |
| pick | checked | stacks | photos |
| nephews | dock | singing | laugh |
| rang | ringing | | |

**High-Frequency Words**

| | |
|---|---|
| month | brother(s) |
| country | happy |

Gramps had a big birthday this month. Mom planned a surprise party. Twins Stephen and Phil were helping.

"We will sort through old photographs of Gramps,"

explained Mom. "We will pick good photos for his party."

Stephen and Phil checked stacks of photos showing Gramps, his brothers and sisters, his kids, grandkids, and nephews. Mom found photos of him from long ago in the country. Stephen felt the best photo showed Gramps fishing on a dock. Phil picked one that showed Gramps singing on stage. The old photos made the twins laugh. They made Mom feel both happy and sad.

Suddenly, a bell rang. It sounded like Mom's phone ringing. No, it was the bell by the door. Stephen looked out the window. It was Gramps!

Phil hid the photos as Gramps came in.

Wow! That was close!

# Photos From Ted

Decodable Practice Reader 24C

Written by Grace Peterson

**Consonant Patterns ph, gh, ck, ng**

| | | | | |
|---|---|---|---|---|
| rings | phone | long | photos | graphs |
| hang | sick | laugh | phrases | back |

**High-Frequency Words**

| | | |
|---|---|---|
| brother | country | long |
| clean | month | |

Jim has an older brother
who is in another country.
Sometimes Ted rings home
on the phone.
Mostly he writes long letters.

Ted works in hard places.
He helps people who need
clean water, food, or money.

Jim has many photos
of Ted riding in jeeps,
reading graphs, looking at maps,
and standing beside huge cliffs.

Ted sends photos of wild animals
for Jim to hang up in his room.
Ted sees bright snakes,
sick birds, and funny bugs.
He has even seen tigers!

When Ted sends Jim a letter, he tells stories that make Jim laugh. He teaches Jim nice phrases to say in that country.

Last month, it rained so much
that Ted's town flooded.
The roads were under water.
"It was hard to go places," Ted wrote.
"But now the roads are clear."

Jim read more good news
in the letter.
Ted is coming back for a visit!
Jim can't wait to be told
Ted's stories in person.

# Fun in August

Written by Maggie Yeom

Decodable Practice Reader 25A

**Vowel Patterns *aw, au, au(gh), al***

| | | | |
|---|---|---|---|
| August | all | baseball | walk |
| always | caught | launch | taller |
| because | fall | falls | thaw |

**High-Frequency Words**

| | |
|---|---|
| stop | best |
| summer | walk |

August is hot!
The sun shines all day.
I cannot stop playing
in the hot, hot sun.

Baseball is the best game
to play in the summer.
We walk or run from base to base.
We always know our team is good.
We win a lot and have fun.

Down at that lake
I caught a fish.
We tried to launch a boat,
but it did not float.
Maybe we'll make a new boat!

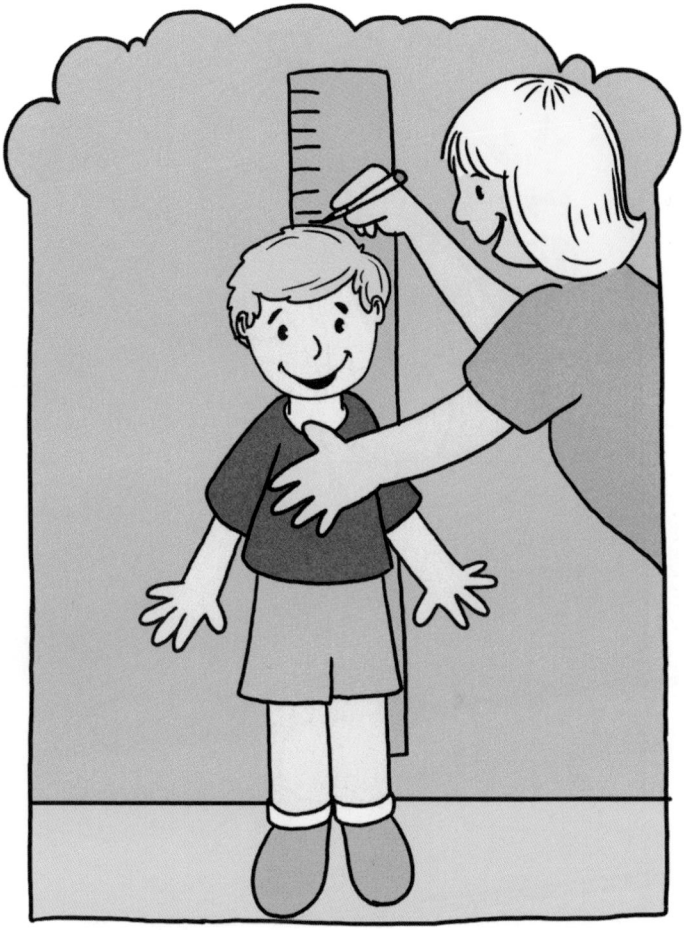

Mom thinks I'm always taller
at the end of a long summer.
I think it's because I run
free on sunny days
through the nice green grass.

When August ends,
fall will start.
First, the winds get cooler.
One leaf falls and then more come
down until no leaves are left.

I wait for the cool fall
and cold winter to pass.
I wait for the snow to melt
and the ground to thaw.

Then it happens.
The sun shines longer.
The grass grows again.
Summer is back!
It's time for more fun in the sun.

# Dawn's Daughter

Decodable Practice Passage 25B

**Vowel Patters *aw, au, au(gh), al***

| | | | |
|---|---|---|---|
| Dawn | daughter | Fawn | crawling |
| walk | taught | lawn | fall |
| sidewalk | talk | ball | caught |
| call | Smalls | calls | paws |
| yawn | | | |

**High-Frequency Words**

| | | |
|---|---|---|
| name | summer | stopped |
| walk | arm | mouth |
| best | | |

Dawn has a daughter. Dawn gave her daughter the name Fawn.

Fawn is just a bit past two years old. This summer, Fawn stopped crawling. Now she can walk! Dawn had taught Fawn to walk on the lawn. That way, Fawn did not fall and get hurt on the sidewalk.

Fawn can talk a bit, too! When Fawn wants a hug, she can say, "Arm!"

When Fawn is hungry, she will say, "Mouth!"

When Fawn wants to play, she will say, "Ball." Fawn has not caught the ball yet, but she tries!

Fawn can call for her pet kitty, Mister Smalls. When Fawn sees Mister Smalls do his trick, Fawn calls, "best kitty!"

Fawn likes to pet Mister Smalls on his paws. But Mister Smalls would rather just yawn and take a nap.

So would Fawn!

# A Job for Paul

Written by April Rydell

Decodable Practice Reader 25C

**Vowel Patterns *aw, au, au(gh), al***

| | | | |
|---|---|---|---|
| Paul | walk | caught | awful |
| paw | taught | paws | because |
| almost | cause | always | naughty |
| small | | | |

**High-Frequency Words**

| | | |
|---|---|---|
| name | tail | rains |
| arm | mouth | |

Rex is my name.
I have a wet nose
and a tail that wags.
Paul is very good to me.

Paul must walk me each day.
He holds my leash
so that it will not get caught.
Even when it rains, we walk.

Paul feeds me twice each day.
When he forgets,
it's not too awful.
I paw gently at his arm
with my dish in my mouth.

Paul taught me a trick.
I stand on two paws
and hold two paws up high.
I am almost as tall as Paul!

Because I'm his dog,
I walk after Paul.
I try to walk softly,
so my paws don't cause noise.

Having me is a hard job.
I am not always so good.
But when I am naughty,
Paul stays calm
and cleans up.

When you think
it's time to get a pet,
just think of Paul and me.
It's no small job having me!

# The Nicest Surprise

Written by Renee McLean

Decodable Practice Reader 26A

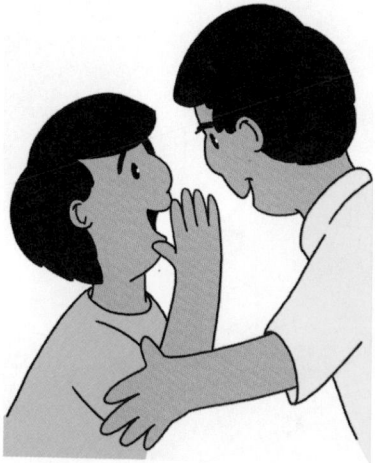

**Inflected Endings *-s, -ed, -ing, -er, -est***

| | | | | |
|---|---|---|---|---|
| longest | planning | biggest | returns | tried |
| excited | helped | prettiest | tied | flowers |
| nicer | soaps | pointed | thinking | cleaned |
| cooking | making | likes | hopped | going |
| waved | faster | cried | rushed | peeking |
| called | closed | opened | nicest | coming |
| hugged | | | | |

**High-Frequency Words**

| | | |
|---|---|---|
| trip | surprise | returns |
| keep | flowers | |

Mom was on the longest trip.
Ben and Jake are planning the
biggest surprise for when she returns.
They have tried to keep it a secret.
They are so excited!

Dad helped Ben gather the
prettiest flowers in the garden.
Ben tied the bundle.
He set his flowers on the table.

Jake put nicer soaps
in Mom's bathroom.
"Maybe she will enjoy a bubble bath,"
Jake pointed out.
"That is good thinking," Ben said.

Jake and Ben cleaned
while Dad was cooking.
"Dad is a good cook," Jake said.
"I hope he is making what Mom likes."
Jake went to talk to Dad.

Dad, Ben, and Jake hopped in the car.
They were going to pick up Mom!
She waved faster at them.
"It's Mom!" Jake and Ben cried.

They rushed home.
"No peeking!" Ben called.
Mom closed her eyes
as Ben and Jake led her inside.
Then she opened her eyes wide.

"This is the nicest surprise!
When I go away, I like coming
home the best!" Mom cried.
Ben and Jake hugged her tightly.

# Zoo Fun

Decodable Practice Passage 26B

**Inflected Endings**

| | | | |
|---|---|---|---|
| handed | printed | words | bigger |
| biggest | animals | exclaimed | smiled |
| added | papers | matches | taller |
| tallest | faster | fastest | shouted |
| slimy | slimier | slimiest | smelly |
| smellier | smelliest | called | looked |
| smiling | | | |

**High-Frequency Words**

trip but might

Miss Bowden's class had a trip to the zoo. Miss Bowden handed each child a sheet of paper. She said, "Each paper has something different printed on it. This paper has the words *big, bigger,* and *biggest animals.*"

"A rhino is the biggest," exclaimed Karen.

Miss Bowden smiled and added, "In the zoo, find animals that best match words on these papers. A rhino is almost the biggest, Karen, but there might be other matches. Write them all on this paper."

The kids read their papers. "Mine has *tall, taller,* and *tallest!*" said Willie.

"*Fast, faster,* and *fastest,*" shouted Eva.

"*Slimy, slimier,* and *slimiest,*" said Ellen with surprise.

"*Smelly, smellier,* and *smelliest!*" called Walt.

The class looked at Miss Bowden with surprise. "You're going to enjoy this day," she said smiling.

# The Happiest King

Written by Calvin Woods

Decodable Practice Reader 26C

**Inflected Endings *-s, -ed, -ing, -er, -est***

| | | | | |
|---|---|---|---|---|
| loneliest | beasts | talking | visits | tried |
| talking | others | scampered | sadder | started |
| crying | skipping | stopped | hopping | cried |
| trusted | biggest | shouted | thrilled | dancing |
| singing | nicest | animals | danced | liked |
| happiest | smiles | thanks | purred | replied |

**High-Frequency Words**

| | |
|---|---|
| king | but |
| ever | afraid |

Lonny was the loneliest.
He is king of this jungle,
but other beasts don't like
talking with him.
Nobody ever visits.

Lonny tried talking to others,
but most just scampered off.
Lonny got sadder and sadder.
He started crying.

Bonny Bunny came skipping by.
She saw Lonny crying.
Bonny felt afraid.
Then she stopped to think.
Why did the king cry?

Bonny started hopping toward Lonny.
"Hello!" she cried.
Lonny trusted Bonny.
He told Bonny how he felt.

"Let's throw the biggest party!"
shouted Bonny.
She was thrilled to help.
"We can plan dancing and singing.
They will see that you are the nicest."

That's what Bonny and Lonny did.
All those animals came.
They danced and sang.
Everyone liked talking with Lonny.
All of them had fun.

Lonny is the happiest king.
Now he smiles and smiles.
"Thanks so much, Bonny!"
Lonny purred.
"Anything to help," she replied.

# Mrs. Jenkins

Written by Hannah Bayer

Decodable Practice Reader 27A

**Abbreviations**

| | |
|---|---|
| Mrs. | St. |
| Rd. | Dr. |
| Ms. | Dec. |
| Mr. | Aug. |
| Ave. | Sept. |

**High-Frequency Words**

| | |
|---|---|
| important | mountain |
| bike | south |

Mrs. Rose Jenkins works at Willis Sign Shop.
Mrs. Jenkins has an important job there.
She is the dot lady.
She paints dots on signs.

What kind of dots?
Have you seen street signs that say "Main St." or "Mountain Rd." or other names?
Mrs. Jenkins painted those dots!

Have you seen mailboxes that say
"Dr. Silva" or "Ms. Smith?"
The dot lady painted those dots, too.
Did she paint your mailbox?

Mrs. Jenkins paints dots on posters, too.
For example, have you seen a poster about a "Dec. 12" music concert?
She may have painted that dot!

Once Mr. Ellis replaced Mrs. Jenkins
with a dot-painting machine.
That was a mistake!
It painted dots in the wrong places!

The machine did not know that "St." meant street or that "Aug." meant August.
Mr. Ellis sold the machine and hired Mrs. Jenkins back.
She was happy.

So if you see a sign that reads "Bike Race! South Maple Ave. closed to traffic on Sept. 15," remember Mrs. Jenkins.
The dot lady may have painted it!

# Titles

Decodable Practice Passage 27B

**Abbreviations**

| | |
|---|---|
| Mrs. | Mr. |
| Dr. | Ms. |
| Nov. | Sep. |

**High-Frequency Words**

| | |
|---|---|
| north | mountain |
| important | almost |

Anthony knew life at North Mountain School was good. But one thing made him unhappy. No one called him by a title!

In his family, his mother had a title. She was called Mrs. Delano. His dad was called Mr. Delano.

His oldest sister was an important doctor, so she was called Dr. Delano. Even his other sister who was almost thirteen was sometimes called Miss Delano. But Anthony was called Anthony or Tony or Delano.

Anthony was thinking about this in class. But Ms. Jones was explaining that month names can be shortened. For example, *Nov.* means November and *Sept.* means September.

Ms. Jones looked at Anthony daydreaming. "Mr. Anthony Delano!" exclaimed Ms. Jones. "Are you listening?"

Anthony was shocked. Ms. Jones called him by a title. But right now, it didn't make him happy!

# North Hall Street

Decodable Practice Reader 27C

Written by Jake Swanson

**Abbreviations**

| | | |
|---|---|---|
| Sat., | Aug. | St. |
| Mr. | Mrs. | Dr. |
| Ms. | Ave. | |

**High-Frequency Words**

north dog almost

A sign said, "Yard Sale on Sat., Aug. 17 at 123 North Hall St." Mr. Walter Hanks saw the sign. He wrote down the day and address.

At home, Mr. Hanks told Mrs. Hanks about the yard sale. Mr. and Mrs. Hanks planned to go. Yard sales were important to them.

Mrs. Hanks took her dog to a vet.
Mrs. Hanks told Dr. Sara Woo
about the sale.
Dr. Woo planned to go.

Dr. Woo told Ms. Nevins.
Hall St. was close to Ms. Nevins' house on Elm Ave.
She planned on going with her family.

Mr. and Mrs. Hanks, Dr. Woo, and Ms. Nevins told more pals.
Almost all of them planned to go to the sale.
They told other people, too.

On Saturday, Mr. and Mrs. Hanks went to the yard sale at 132 South Hall St.
So did all a lot of other people.
But there was no yard sale!

Mr. Hanks looked at his note.
"Whoops, it's not 132, but 123
North Hall St.," he said.
And that is where all the shoppers
went!

# My Future

Written by Greg Morton

Decodable Practice Reader 28A

**Final Syllables *-tion, -ture***

| | | |
|---|---|---|
| future | picture(s) | mixture |
| action | stations | nation |
| locations | nature | motion |

**High-Frequency Words**

| | | |
|---|---|---|
| might | paint | smile |
| move | take | |

There are many jobs
that people have.
When I think about my future,
I try to picture what I might be.
I have many choices!

Maybe I will be an artist.
I can paint fine pictures,
using a mixture of colors.
My pictures will make people smile.

Maybe I will be a firefighter.
I can take action to protect my city.
Maybe I will work at stations
all over the nation!

Maybe I will be a builder.
I can make skyscrapers
and houses in many locations.
I could even make a house for myself!

Maybe I will be a park ranger.
I can see wild animals and enjoy nature.
I will show people how to be safe and keep things clean in my park.

Maybe I will be a dancer.
I will be in motion every day.
I will dance in shows
and teach kids
how to move nicely.

My future might hold anything!
I know that I will be happy
if I do something that I like
and that makes other people glad.

# Future Profession

Decodable Practice Passage 28B

**Final Syllables *-tion, -ture, ion***

| | | |
|---|---|---|
| conclusion | future | questions |
| pasture | sections | nature |
| discussion | pictures | locations |
| nation | action | profession |

**High-Frequency Words**

| | | |
|---|---|---|
| take | paint | sections |
| move | nation | action |
| smile | | |

What am I going to be when I grow up? I am just seven. So I can take a lot of time to reach a conclusion. Still I like thinking about the future. I like asking myself questions about what I might do.

For example, should I be a farmer and work in a pasture? Or I might be good at house painting. I would paint top sections first and move down. Or I might be a park ranger. I like nature and hiking.

After a bit of discussion with mom and dad, I decided I might be a photographer. I snap good pictures. As an adult, I might travel to different locations in this nation and take photos of people and action that I see. Photography just might be the right profession for me.

Smile and say cheese!

# Action at the Game

Decodable Practice Reader 28C

Written by Kelley Fulsom

**Final Syllables *-tion, -ture***

| | | | | |
|---|---|---|---|---|
| station | section | caution | nation | mentioned |
| action | motion | captured | picture | future |

**High-Frequency Words**

| | | |
|---|---|---|
| left | found | section |
| nation | action | team |
| ball | | |

My sister is taking me
to my first football game.
I can hardly wait!

We left the station
and walked to the school.
We found our seats
in the lower section.

"Why do those players have on such big shirts?" I asked.
"There are pads under them," my sister replied. "The players must use caution so that they don't get hurt."

"This team is one of the best
in the nation," my sister mentioned.
I can tell that she is proud
of her school's team.

We saw lots of action
in this game.
It was hard to see it all
because the motion was so fast.

We saw action in the stands too. Fans clapped and yelled for each team. When our team captured the ball and won, my sister jumped up and hugged me.

We took a picture
with the winning players.
When I see that picture in the
future, it will remind me of the fun
we had.

# Helpless Randy

Written by Liz Hornby

Decodable Practice Reader 29A

**Suffixes *-ness, -less, -able, -ible***

| | | | |
|---|---|---|---|
| lovable | useless | collectible | helpless |
| darkness | sadness | kindness | goodness |
| sweetness | weakness | fixable | brightness |
| colorless | | | |

**High-Frequency Words**

| | |
|---|---|
| without | life |
| please | back |

This is moving day.
Sandy did not grab Randy,
her old lovable bunny doll,
when she ran out the door.

"Did you pack that bunny?"
Mom asked Sandy.
"He's not old and useless.
He might be a collectible."

"Randy is helpless without me!"
Sandy cried.
"Without me his life will be filled
with darkness and sadness."

"Please show kindness," Sandy begged. "Let me go back for my bunny. "Mom's goodness shone through. She smiled because of Sandy's sweetness.

"You know my weakness,"
Mom laughed.
"This is fixable.
We will go get Randy."

Sandy picked up Randy and
hugged him.
Brightness had come back to her face.
"We'll make you new clothes,"
she said.
"Your old ones are colorless."

Sandy got in the car
and set Randy on her lap.
Mom smiled.
Mom knew that Sandy would have
missed her good friend.

# An Incredible Visit

Decodable Practice Passage 29B

**Suffixes *-ness, -less, -able, -ible***

horrible darkness sleepless useless
painless restless terrible spotless
brightness kindness possible toothless
remarkable

**High-Frequency Words**

please no stay
small lights feel
back

It was time for my trip to the dentist. I felt afraid. A dentist visit was a horrible thing. The night before, in the darkness of my bedroom, I spent a sleepless night.

That morning, I told Mom, "Please don't make me go!"

But it was useless. "No, Jane," Mom explained. "It will be painless. And I'll stay right with you!"

I was restless on the drive. "Don't be afraid," smiled Mom. "Dr. Ames is not a terrible person!"

Dr. Ames' place was small and spotless. The brightness of the lights was slightly blinding, but Dr. Ames was filled with kindness. In no time, my checkup was over. Was it possible? I didn't feel a thing! And I was afraid I would end up toothless! Now I can't wait to go back! Isn't that remarkable?

# In the Darkness

Written by Joel Grand

Decodable Practice Reader 29C

**Suffixes *-ness, -less, -able, -ible***

| | | | |
|---|---|---|---|
| remarkable | useless | restless | darkness |
| dependable | brightness | helpless | readable |
| sleepless | kindness | edible | |

**High-Frequency Words**

| | | |
|---|---|---|
| power | no | lights |
| small | feel | stay |

There was a remarkable storm.
It knocked out our power.
We had no lights.
Many things in our house
became useless.

We felt restless in the darkness.
We went to look for things to do.
We found something that helped
us in the darkness.

Mom found a dependable flashlight.
The light was small, but its
brightness made us feel brave.
Mom and I went to explore.

"We are not helpless," Mom added.
"We have light, and we have
each other, so we're not lonely.
Let's find something readable."

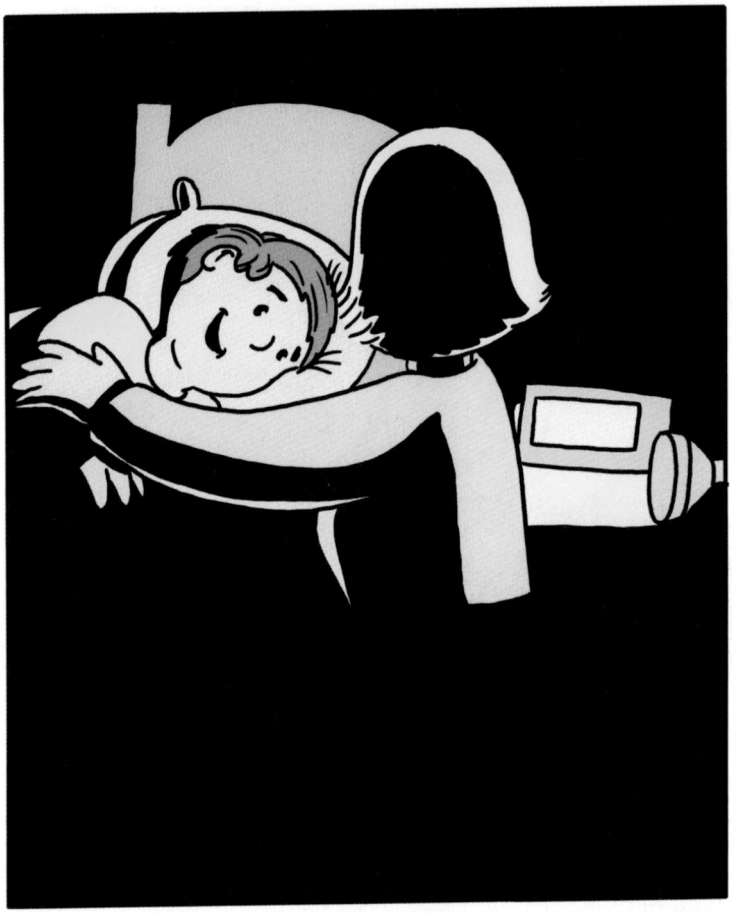

When it was bedtime, Mom and I
went to my room.
I was sleepless.
My nightlight did not glow.
Mom stayed with me.

Mom was still in my room
when I woke.
"Why did you stay?" I asked.
"I didn't want you to be afraid,"
she said.

As I hugged Mom for her kindness, I saw that the clock blinked on and off. "Our power is on," Mom cried. "No more staying in the darkness! Let's find something edible!"

# Hiking the Hard Way

Written by Lynn South

Decodable Practice Reader 30A

**Prefixes *micro-, mid-, mis-, non-***

| | | |
|---|---|---|
| mismatched | midway | mislaid |
| misstep | microscope | midstream |
| nonstop | midday | misplaced |

**High-Frequency Words**

| | | |
|---|---|---|
| wrong | right | were |
| start | stream | |

Danny was so excited!
His scout troop was going hiking.
He loaded his backpack.
But things started going wrong
right away.

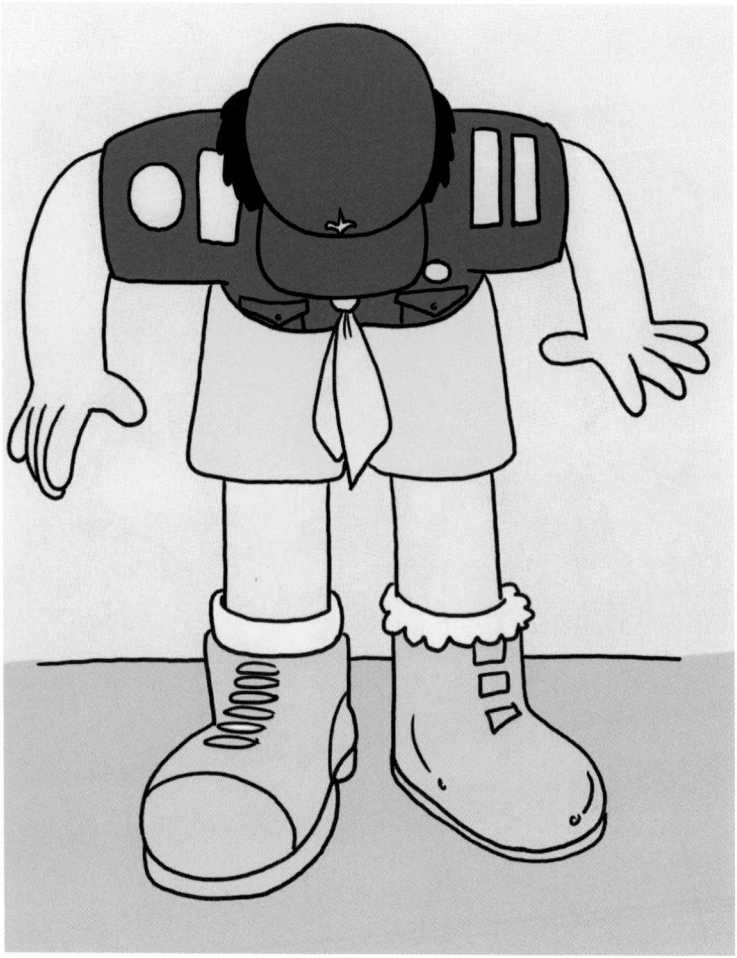

Danny put on his boots
in the darkness.
When he got on the bus,
Danny looked down.
His boots were mismatched!

Midway through the bus trip,
Danny cried, "No, no!"
He had mislaid his water bottle.
It was not in his backpack.
"I have two bottles," Kim said.

At the start of that hike,
they crossed a stream.
Danny took a misstep
and slipped midstream.
Splash! Danny broke his microscope.

Danny dried off, and they hiked nonstop.
The hikers stopped at midday for lunch.
Danny was happy to stop.

He looked in his backpack
for his sack lunch.
"I misplaced my lunch!"
Danny cried.
"It must still be on our bus."

Kim gave him part of her lunch.
Then they hiked back.
"I like hiking," Danny said
when he was safe on the bus.
"But it seems that hiking doesn't
like me."

# Wrong!

Decodable Practice Passage 30B

**Prefixes mis-, mid-, non-, micro**

| | | |
|---|---|---|
| midwinter | nonstop | midnight |
| Midtown | midway | misread |
| mistake | nonsense | misprint |
| microfilm | misleading | misinformation |

**High-Frequency Words**

| | | |
|---|---|---|
| check | latest | wrong |
| started | can't | right |
| which | | |

In midwinter, Ann enjoyed reading by her family's fireplace. At times, she stayed up reading nonstop until midnight! So she liked to check out books on Midtown School bookshelves.

The latest book Ann read was about the United States. Midway through the book, she saw something wrong. It said that the Pony Express was started in 1960! Did Ann misread that? No, it was mistake!

"This can't be right!" she thought. "The Pony Express started in 1860, not 1960! That's nonsense!"

Ann knew this was a misprint. Ann took the book back to Midtown School. Miss Shelly was by the microfilm. "Miss Shelly, this book is misleading." Ann said. "Can you spot which date on this page is a misprint?"

Miss Shelly spotted the mistake. "Thanks, Ann," Miss Shelly grinned. "We can't have misinformation on these shelves!"

# The Midtown Market Sale

Decodable Practice Reader 30C

Written by Lisa Vollmer

**Prefixes *micro-, mid-, mis-, non-***

| | | |
|---|---|---|
| midtown | midday | microwave |
| nonsense | misprint | misleading |
| midyear | midweek | midnight |

**High-Frequency Words**

| | | |
|---|---|---|
| shop | can't | check |
| which | late | |

Jane and her dad went
to Midtown Market to shop
at midday on Sunday.
They found a good sale
on microwaves and shirts.

Dad looked at a tag.
"This price can't be right.
This is nonsense.
I've never seen shirts this cheap!"

The clerk came by.
"I will check," she said.
"It might be a misprint,
which would be misleading."
She went to ask her boss.

That clerk came back smiling.
"It is right," she said.
"This midyear sale
has good prices."

Jane and Dad looked for other
good deals.
Then Dad looked at the clock.
"We have to pick up Mom,"
he said.
"We will be late if we don't go now."

"Maybe we can return midweek,"
Jane said.
"This sale ends at midnight,"
the clerk noted.
Dad looked again at that cheap shirt.

"Mom will want to see
these good deals," he noted.
"We will bring her here
while these prices are low."